# Pioneer

# Free Will Baptists

# Ministers

# Burial Locations

# In

# New York

Copyright 2016
By
Dr. Alton E. Loveless

ISBN 978-1523632398 Soft cover

2020 Update

This book was printed in the United States of America.

To order additional copies of this book, contact:
FWB Publications
Enchanting Acres
1006 Rayme Drive
Columbus, Ohio 43207
Alton.loveless@prodigy.net
Or
www.amazon.com

**FWB**
FWB Publications

## Introduction

## New York

This book represents all that were part of the Free Will Baptist movement, consisting of the Palmer (south), Randall (north) and others such as the Stone, John-Thomas, John Wheeler Assns., NC OFWB and more.

Many of the photos are poor quality, but it was all I could find. Likewise, I do not have photos or tombstones for many of them. The information about these ministers were all that was available to me or found in archives. I made every effort to include those for which they would be remembered. Some I had no information, but research had shown they were of our denomination.

This Section is taken for a two Volume set done by this author.

# PIONEER FREE WILL BAPTISTS MINISTERS BURIAL LOCATIONS IN NEW YORK

## New York

**Asa G Abbott**
Birth:
Sep. 11, 1803
Death:
Feb. 11, 1877
German, N. Y.
Burial:
Westview Cemetery
German Four Corners,
Chenango County, New York

Abbott, Rev. A. G., a native of Pennsylvania. He entered the ministry with the Methodists at an early age, but later moved to Chenango Co., N. Y., and spent the last twenty years of his ministry with the Free Baptists of the McDonough. M. His faith in God survived many afflictions. He was an earnest, thoughtful preacher,

and his wise counsels had a wide influence among his brethren by whom he was venerated.

**Adon Aldrich**
Birth:
Jul. 22, 1795
Uxbridge
Worcester County,
Massachusetts
Death:
Jul. 20, 1853
Ashford
Cattaraugus County,
New York
Burial:
Bond Cemetery
Springville
Cattaraugus County,
New York

He was a minister in the Ontario quarterly meeting in New York State. In 1827 went to Chenango County, where he preached and established the Norwich and New Berlin churches.

**John J Allen**
Birth:
1822
Death:
May 26, 1899
Burial:
Old Depauville Cemetery
Depauville
Jefferson County,
New York

He was educated at Whitestown Seminary and Biblical School. He began to preach in 1849 and was ordained in September 1853. He baptized about 300 converts during his ministry in the area where he had served so long. For 20 years he served as the clerk and treasurer of the Jefferson Quarterly Meeting and had been a delegate to one of the General Conferences.

Albert A. Armstrong
Birth:
1848
Cuba, Allegany County, New York
Death:
1937
Great Valley,
Cattaraugus County,
New York
Burial:
Willoughby Cemetery,
Great Valley,
Cattaraugus County, New York

Albert was educated at the Pike Seminary in Tenbroeck, New York. He received his license to preach in the Free Will Baptist Church in 1869. The year after his conversion, he was ordained by the Cattaraugus Quarterly Meeting June 11, 1878. Except for a few years in Pennsylvania around 1900, his ministry was continued in Western New York State.

*As A Well-Spent Day Brings Happy Sleep, So A Life Well Used Brings Happy Death.*

**Dr George Harvey Ball**
Birth:
Dec. 7, 1819
Sherbrooke, Canada
Death:
Feb. 20, 1907
Burial:
Forest Lawn Cemetery
Buffalo
Erie County, New York
Plot: Section 3

Ball, who was the son of William and Marcy (Harvey) Ball, had his early days in Massachusetts. In 1836 they removed to Ohio, where, while making a home in the wilderness for the family, his used the time to study systematically the evenings until ten o'clock, under the guidance of his mother, and when twenty years of age commenced teaching. During that winter Rev. Ransom Dunn, holding meetings in the schoolhouse, said to him, "Do you think it reasonable and right to serve God?" "Yes," he replied. "And you aim to be a reasonable man do you not?" "Most certainly." "Then you will serve God of course," said the preacher, and passed on. The appeal to reason prevailed, where other appeals had failed. After about two years at Farmington Academy, he spent two years more at Grand River Institute, and preached occasionally in the vicinity, receiving license to preach from the Ashtabula Q.M. in 1843. The next year he went to Ontario, Can., to teach, but was kept constantly at preaching for more than a year, and enjoyed several revivals. He then attended the Biblical School at Whitestown, graduating in 1847. The following year he was married to Maria L. Bensly and entered upon a three years' pastorate at Chester, O. A part of this time he was principal of Geauga Seminary, and numbered James A. Garfield among his pupils. In 1851 he went to Buffalo, N. Y., to plant a church. After four years he settled with the Roger Williams church,

Providence, R. I., but soon returned to Buffalo to save the interest there. In 1870 he became New York editor of *The Morning Star,* and the next year editor of the *Baptist Union.* In 1877 he returned to Buffalo Where he still remains pastor of a flourishing church planted by himself. Bro. Ball has always been a diligent student and an indefatigable worker. He received the degree of Doctor of Divinity from Bates College, Me. He has published several small books of merit, and wrote extensively for the religious and secular press. As a preacher he is argumentative, pungent and direct; as a pastor, sympathetic and helpful. He had a wide influence in the denomination, having served as Trustee of Storer College from its foundation, and of Hillsdale College also, except one term; and being now a member of the Foreign Mission and Conference Boards. In 1886 he visited the General Baptists of England, for the General Conference. His daughter Julia was a graduate of Packer College, Brooklyn, N. Y.,. and Ella J., since completed the Classical Course at Hillsdale College, and for some eight years was lady-principal of Pike Seminary, N. Y.

**Rev Laban Eli Bates**
Birth:
Jul. 10, 1820
Ellisburg
Jefferson County
New York
Death:
Aug. 14, 1896
Fabius
Onondaga County
New York
Burial:
Fabius Evergreen Cemetery
Fabius
Onondaga County
New York

Rev. Laban Eli Bates, son of Liberty

and Mary (Russell) Bates, was born July 10, 1820. He was led to Christ in 1838, began to preach in 1844, and was ordained in 1849. He first united with the Congregational church in Norway, NY, but was soon baptized and has since taught and practiced baptism by immersion. He engaged in evangelistic work with success, and later ministered to the West Camden church eleven years, and the Florence and Redfield church five years. In 1871, he united with the Free Baptists, and has been pastor at Fabius five years at Potter four years, Cowlesville three years, and at Marilla, six years, the last four begin devoted exclusively to the Marilla church. In these fields his labors have been blessed of God.

Bro. Bates has always taken advanced positions on all moral questions. As an abolitionist, he voted for Birney, with the "third party"; and in temperance work he is a staunch prohibitionist.

Feb. 19, 1849, he married Caroline D. Bronson, who passed to rest May 30, 1868. Their oldest son, since deceased, graduated from Cornell University; Charles P. practices law at Sioux Falls, Dak; Carrie is a missionary in New York City, and the four other daughters have engaged in teaching.

Sept. 19, 1874, he married Anne S. Dudley of Kingsfield, Maine.

### Velorus Beebe
Birth:
Sep. 10, 1810
Cuba, Allegany County,
New York
Death:
May 28, 1879
Friendship,
Allegany County, New York
Burial:
Richburg Cemetery,
Richburg, Allegany County,
New York

He commenced preaching at 18 years of age in Yates County. Travelling as an evangelist he held meetings in many places in Ohio and Michigan. After this he ministered to the church in Bradford, New York, fourteen years; in E. Troy, Pennsylvania, two years; in Veteran, New York, two years, and Wert and Boliver fourteen years. Revivals, some quite extensive in these places. He represented the New York and Pennsylvania Y.M.in the General Conferences of 1847 and 1850.

### Rev Justus L Bingham
Birth:
1819
Death:
Jan. 21, 1853
Summerhill
Cayuga County
New York, USA
Burial:
Indian Mound Cemetery
Moravia
Cayuga County, New York

Rev. Justus L. Bingham, was suddenly killed at Summer Hill, N.Y., about 1853. He was ordained by the Jefferson Quarterly Meeting, in 1845, and labored in that vicinity for a time, and later in the south part of the state.

A native NY Freewill Baptist minister, ordained in 1845. He died young from an accident.

*What is your life? You are a mist that appears for a little while and then vanishes" (James 4:14b).*

### Rev Elijah F. Bliven
Birth:
Jun. 30, 1815
Death:
Sep. 11, 1894
Burial:
Rogersville Forest Lawn Cemetery
Dansville
Steuben County
New York
Plot: SD 13

Ordained in 1848 by the Methodist Episcopal church, and united with the Free Baptists in 1873. He worked in revivals and building of several churches.

### Rev Charles Bowles
Birth:
1761
Boston
Suffolk County
Massachusetts
Death:
Mar. 16, 1843
Malone
Franklin County
New York
Burial:
Constable Cemetery
Constable
Franklin County
New York

Located through Northern New York Tombstone Transcriptions.

Erected to the memory of Rev. Charles BOWLES. A Soldier of the Revolution and for more than 40 years a successful Minister of one Gospel in the Freewill Baptist Connection. He departed this life in Malone, March 16, 1843, AE 82 Y'rs.

Elder Bowles was the founding pastor of a number of Baptist churches in Vermont. His biography can be read on line.
John W. Lewis, The Life,Labors, and Travels of Elder Charles Bowles, of the Free Will Baptist Denomination, (Watertown MA, 1852). Submitted by Rev. John Burbank, clerk of the First Baptist Church of Starksboro VT

At the age of twenty-one he professed religion, and united with the Hamburg, N. Y., church. Soon after his marriage to Miss Fanny Perham, in 1841, he moved to Boston, N. Y., and in l848 to Dayton. He was ordained in 1860. His ministry was confined to the Cattaraugus and Erie Q. M's and was characterized by earnestness, fidelity and self-sacrifice. Aged 69 years 19 days

**Nathaniel Brown**
Birth:
Apr. 7, 1765,
Warren
Litchfield County,
Connecticut
Death:
Sep. 2, 1844
Bethany Center,
Genesee County,
New York
Burial:
West Bethany Cemetery,
West Bethany,
Genesee County,
New York,
Plot: New Section

**Daniel Brown**
Birth:
Unknown
Death:
Aug. 5, 1882
Dayton, N. Y.
Burial:
Parklawn Cemetery
Wesley, Cattaraugus County,
New York

He was ordained by the Stratford Association June 27, 1802 and after six years of successful ministry moved in 1808 to Bethany, New York where he purchased a large tract of land and build a sawmill and grist mill. He organized the Bethany Church, the first Free Will Baptist Church west of the Genesee river and remained its pastor until his death for a period of 30 years. Besides this work in New York, he assisted in the organization of the Ohio yearly meeting. He was a prominent member of the first Gen. Conference and did much to shape the policy for its future years. Nathaniel was a Revolutionary War veteran. He Enlisted in the Strafford, Orange County, Vermont.

**Rev Adam B. Bullock**
Birth:
Jul. 9, 1806, USA
Death:

Apr. 14, 1848
Montgomery County
New York
Burial:
Morris Family Burial Ground
Ames
Montgomery County
New York

Rev. Adam B. Bullock, died aged 41 years. He was converted sixteen years before, attended Hamilton Theological Seminary, spent some time in teaching, and was ordained in 1841.

He labored with the Canajoharie and Ames churches, saw many additions, and was much respected. His gentleness of spirit endeared him to the people. His loss was deeply felt.

**Rev Benjamin Bundy**
Birth:
1796
Connecticut
Death:
Aug. 25, 1870
Burial:
River View Cemetery
Willisville
St. Lawrence County, New York

He was a native of Conn, d. in W. Parishville, NY, aged 74 years. He was converted in Randolph, VT, and at age 25, mar. Miss Betsey Kibber. He soon began to preach, and was ordained by Elders Kimball and Hall, in Bershire, VT.
Inscription:
Age 74

## William C Byer

Birth:
1814
Eaton
Madison County, New York
Death:
Oct. 30, 1868
Fabius
Onondaga County, New York
Burial:
Fabius Evergreen Cemetery
Fabius, Onondaga County,
New York

Rev. Byer, Sr., was a native of Eaton, NY. While attending school in Clinton (NY) he became acquainted with Miss Samantha Ward, who became his wife and helper through life. Her influence was instrumental in leading him to Christ.He was ordained in 1842 to the Freewill Baptist ministry, and labored in Union Yearly Meeting until about 1856, when he became connected with the Burlington Flats Church. He held many protracted meetings and baptized, during his ministry, about five hundred converts. As a preacher he was warm-hearted and earnest. He never feared to rebuke sin, yet was kind and benevolent.The son, William C., Jr., also became a Free Baptist minister. He mar. Inez K. Smith Oct. 18, 1876. He was educated at Whitestown Seminary and received ordination in 1883, taking charge of the North Scriba FB church, where he continued some years. He enjoyed the esteem of his people.

## Elder Chester Chaffee

Birth:
Oct. 7, 1791
Death:
Sep. 5, 1876
Arcade, N. Y.
Burial:
Arcade Rural Cemetery
Arcade, Wyoming County,
New York

Chaffee, a native of Grafton, Vt., died at age 85 years. In 1816 he moved to Boston, N. Y., where he served the church as deacon. After fourteen years he moved to Arcade, receiving ordination in 1832, and was connected with the China, Hume and Elton churches. He was a reliable man, faithfulto the trusts committed to him. Parents: David Chaffee (1765–1835) and Anna Johnson (1771–1827)1st Spouse: Abigail __ (1793–1827)2nd Spouse: Mrs. Lydia Jackson (?-1869)

## Daniel Chase

Birth:
Unknown
Death:
Mar. 2, 1850
Mount Pleasant, NY
Burial:
West Windsor Cemetery
West Windsor
Broome County, New York

Rev. Daniel Chase, born about 1771-72, and died at age 79 years.He began his ministry about 1800, Elder Randall assisting in his ordination. He labored in New Hampshire and Vermont, and in 1816, removed to Jackson, Pennsylvania, being, it is thought, the first minister of the denomination to settle in that state. He rendered faithful service in Susquehanna and Wayne Counties, Pennsylvania, and in Broome County, New York. He represented the Gibson Q.M. Pennsylvania at the organization of the Susquahanna Yearly Meeting.

---

## Elbridge Gerry Cilley

Birth:
Feb. 19, 1821
Danbury
Merrimack County
New Hampshire
Death:
Dec. 26, 1901
Bolton
Warren County
New York
Burial:

Cilley - Pratt
Warren County
New York, USA

Elbridge Cilley, aged about eighty years, a resident of Bolton, died Saturday, at the home of his son-in-law, Lawrence Pratt. Mr. Cilley was twice married. His first wife was Miss Sylvia Phelps (1825-69); his second. Mrs. Nancy Hill Bidwell (1830-). He Is survived by three sons and one daughter, Frank, Fremont and Stephen Cilley and Mrs. Lawrence Pratt, all of Bolton. Deceased is also survived by four step-daughters, Mrs. Jane Ann Turner, Mrs. Alexander Pratt. Mrs. Samuel Harrington and Miss Belle Bidwell, The funeral was held Saturday at the Lamb school house.
Grave unmarked

Parents:
Stephen Cilley (1798 - 1861)
Cyrene King Cilley (1801 - 1863)
Spouse:
Nancy H. Hill Cilley (1830 - 1895)
Children:
Benjamin Cilley (1846 - 1917)*
Frank P. Cilley (1853 - 1908)*
Fremont Cilley (1857 - 1937)*
Adeline Cilley Pratt (1859 - 1943)*
Sibling:
Elbridge Gerry Cilley (1821 - 1901)
Serena K Cilley Pratt (1832 - 1860)*

### Ardon Cobb
Birth:
1802
New York, USA
Death:
Aug. 10, 1868
Burial:
Overackers Cemetery
Middlesex,
Yates County,
New York

He became a minister after a conversion in 1833, ordained 1840. His labors were with the Danville, Middlesex, North Potter, Sparta, Italy, Scottsburg and Jerusalem churches. He was earnest and active in the work. The Middlesex church especially was blessed under his efforts. His devotion found expression in the frequent inquiry, "How can I render the most efficient service to Christ?".-

### Isaiah Bangs Coleman
Birth:
Mar. 7, 1809
Stephentown
Rensselaer County,
New York
Death:
Mar. 14, 1883
West Stephentown
Rensselaer County,
New York
Burial:
Hillside Cemetery
Stephentown,
Rensselaer County,
New York

Coleman died of paralysis at his home age 74 years. He was converted when but a boy, and baptized by Rev. John Allen. His facilities for education were limited, but his studious habits and thirst for knowledge soon prepared him to serve as a teacher for ten years; an advantage to himself, as well as others. May 1, 1834, he married Miss Ann V. Dunham, his companion through life. May 10 of the same year he was licensed to preach, and March 25, 1835, was ordained. He labored with the old Stephentown and Sand Lake churches until Jan. 6, 1844, when he became pastor of the West Stephentown church, then having fifty-eight members. He remained its pastor thirty-nine years, and left it at his death a flourishing church of 180 members, a living testimony to the faithful service rendered. Of those who united with his own church, he baptized 225, besides many who went to other churches. It is said that he married over fourteen hundred couples. Few ministers have attended more funerals than he. His charities were generous and frequent. He was a strong advocate of temperance and all virtues. His modest, unassuming spirit, together with home duties, confined his helpful influence to narrower limits, though he served as delegate to the General Conference a number of times. On March 3 he told his wife he had had a shock, and could be with her but a short time. In less than an hour his power of speech was gone, and in a few days a vast multitude gathered around his bed, attesting the high esteem in which he was held by the community. He was a teacher, storekeeper, postmaster and minister of the Church he helped found.

### Ashel J Cooley
Birth:
July 6, 1826.
Death:
Sep. 25, 1905
Point Peninsula
Jefferson County,
N. Y.
Burial:
Woodlawn Cemetery
Elmira
Chemung County,
New York

He was married in September, 1846, to Miss Rachel Leonard, and in January, 1865, was baptized, uniting with the Three-Mile Bay church, of which his wife was a member. He was ordained June 7, 1874, by the Jefferson Q. M., and was pastor of the Three-Mile Bay church a brief period. He has since served as city missionary at Ithaca, N. Y., in 1880, and as pastor at Dryden, 1881-83; at Stephentown Center, 1883-85, and for a time at Hadley. Died at 82 yrs, 10 mos, 3days Utica, NY

### Rev Oliver L. Cooper
Birth:
Oct. 10, 1846
New York
Death:
1933
Burial:
Riverview Cemetery
Oxford
Chenango County
New York

Served in the military, and afterward, ordained to the ministry March 13, 1881. He was a pastor in German, Willet, and East McDonough churches.

In 1871, he was married to Carrie Blanchard. They had the following children:

### Amos Daniels
Birth:
Aug. 23, 1787
Hartford,
Hartford County,
Connecticut
Death:
Apr. 29, 1873
Burial:
Vestal Park Cemetery,
Vestal,
Broome County, New York

He worked with the Methodists as a licensed preacher, but because of his views on baptism they did not ordain him, and he united with the Free Baptists, receiving ordination at the Owego Q.M. in 1822. He was pastor of the Virgil and Dryden church twenty-five years, reorganized the Dryden church and was its pastor twelve years; organized the Fabius church and was its pastor several years and was also pastor at Jackson, East Troy and other points. He labored extensively in the Susquehanna Yearly Meeting as an evangelist, witnessing many revivals during his ministry. His ministry was over 51 years, and full of usefulness.

### Freeman Darte
Birth:
1804
Death:
Jan. 22, 1883
Yorkshire,
Cattaraugus County, New York
Burial:
Delevan Cemetery,
Delevan,
Cattaraugus County, New York

He lived in the Cattaraugus, Yorkshire, area, and farmed to support his family. Freeman was a member, clerk, and then preacher of The First Free Will Baptist Church of East Randolph, NY. He consecrated his life to Christ in 1832, was licensed to preach about 1837 and ordained about 1842, in the Freewill Baptist Church. He was a faithful minister, laboring with good acceptance in many churches of the Erie and Cattaraugus Q.M.'s.

### Ira Day
Birth:
Oct. 6, 1818
Burlington, New York
Death:
Jul. 29, 1883
Fabius, New York
Burial:
Willet Cemetery
Willet, Cortland County,
New York

He was converted when thirteen years of age, and joined the Free Baptists soon after moving to Willet, in 1856. He soon began to preach, and ultimately became pastor of the Willet church. Three years before at his death he settled with the Fabius church, which was blessed under his labors. He was a devoted Christian, giving his service and his wealth to the Lord. A gift of $500 to the Norwich church is worthy of special notice. The Central Association, of which he was a trustee, honored him with resolutions of esteem. Spouse: Susannah Whitmore Day (1818 - 1880).

Inscription:
For we know if our earthly house of this tabernacle were dissolved, we have a building of God an house not made with hands, eternal in the heavens.
2 Corinthians 5:1

### Zebulon Dean
Birth:
1779
New York
Death:

Dec. 4, 1883
Yates County, New York
Burial:
Evergreen Cemetery, Dresden,
Yates County, New York

Zebulon settled early in Yates Co., and was ordained a Free Will Baptist minister in 1813, probably in Benton church. It's influence and interest extended over a territory of forty miles in diameter along the western shores of Lake Seneca. He pastored that church and at Barrington in 1829, a church he helped organize in 1819. His ministry was in the surrounding towns and villages In 1819, he with Samuel WIRE, then a licensed preacher, heard that David Marks, a boy preacher of fifteen, was in need of spiritual consolation at Junius, so they went thirty miles and encouraged David and baptized him July 11. Marks was soon afterwards associated in revival meetings with Rev. Dean, who had helped him. In 1829, Rev. Dean attended the third General Conference, at Spafford, N.Y.

# Behold I Come Quickly And Every Eye Shall See Me!

**Rev Jacob Decker**
Birth:
1808
Death:
Jan. 12, 1865
Buena Vista, N. Y

Burial:
Baker Farm Cemetery
Canisteo
Steuben County
New York

He was a native of Spencer, N. Y., and experienced religion at Urbana in 1830. He soon began to preach and was ordained in 1835. He spent most of his ministerial life as an itinerant in southwestern New York and northern Pennsylvania, where he saw much of God's power in the quickening of professors and in the conversion of sinners. He was a man of an excellent spirit.

**Manoah Delling**
Birth:
1782
New Hampshire
Death:
Jul. 30, 1851
Wayne County, New York
Burial:
Zurich Cemetery
Arcadia
Wayne County, New York

Manoah was a Baptist minister who eventually settled in Lyons, NY Ordained in New York soon after 1820, and labored there in the Free Baptist church.

### Oscar Hanning Denney

Birth:
Jul. 10, 1860
Gallia County, Ohio
Death:
Jan. 7, 1945
Canandaigua
Ontario County, New York
Burial:
Borden-Elk Creek Cemetery
Borden
Steuben County, New York

He was born near Rio Grande, Ohio and was converted in 1869 after which he pursued studies at Rio Grande college and for a season at Hillsdale in Michigan. He received his license to preach in 1879 and was ordained on December 17, 1882. He pastored a number of churches in Ohio before moving to the state of New York where several revivals attended his labors. He also assisted in the organizing of four churches.

### Amasa Dodge

Birth:
1768
New London County, Connecticut
Death:
Aug. 13, 1850
Lewis County, New York

Burial:
West Lowville Rural Cemetery
West Lowville
Lewis County, New York

He was ordained that Lowville, New York, April 4, 1818. He was an exhorter rather than a sermonizer; a true man, devoted to the cause of the Master, yet conservative; and when the Free Communion Baptists united with the Free Will Baptist, he, almost alone opposed the union, yet his integrity was never questioned.

### Asa Dodge

Birth:
Apr. 14, 1799
Ludlow, Hampden County, Massachusetts
Death:
Aug. 2, 1877
New York

Burial:
Nanticoke Valley Cemetery
Union Center, Broome County,
New York

Rev. Asa Dodge was the son of Asa and Sarah Dodge--one of four sons who were Freewill Baptists ministers [Edward E., Gurley, Calvin and Asa] In 1806, this family settled in New Concord (now Lisbon) N.H. At age 13 yrs, with his brother Edward E, he conducted meetings in which several were converted. He was baptized by Rev. J. Quinby and united with Sugar Hill Church. He attended Morse Academy in Hanover four years, when his family moved to NY. He then entered upon the active life of the ministry. He was licensed by Owego Quarterly Meeting in 1821, and ordained the next year. The first Free Baptist meeting in Troy, NY was held by him in 1822. The Owega QM owes much to him for its prosperity, where most of his ministry was spent. His influence was felt in other QM's as well. He was a successful minister and many souls were converted through his agency.

He occupied a prominent position in the denomination, having represented the Susquehanna, NY Yearly Meeting (YM) in the General Conference of 1829 and several times later. The last ten years of his life was laid aside by infirmities, but he rejoiced in the assurance of a bright home above.

**Jacob Hilton Durkee**
Birth:
Apr. 30, 1847
Yarmouth
Nova Scotia, Canada
Death:
1925
Monroe County, New York
Burial:
Riverside Cemetery
Rochester
Monroe County, New York
Plot: Sect. M.

Rev. Durkee, was born of Free Baptist parents in Yarmouth Co. Nova Scotia. April 30, 1847. He was converted when about nineteen years of age, and soon entered the New Hampton Institution, N.H., graduating in 1871. Subsequently, he studied about a year in the theological department of Bates College [Maine]. He was ordained a Free Baptist minister at Meredith, N.H., Sept. 28, 1871; a properous pastorate at that place followed. Later he gathered the Free Baptist church of Halifax, N.S., which secured a house of worship under his labors. After supplying the New Market, N.H,, church for a season he went to New York in 1877, where his four years labor at Phoenix and three at Pike resulted in strengthening these churches. He also aided in organizing the Bliss church. In 1884, under direction of the Central Ass'n., he opened a mission at Batavia (NY) which is growing into permanence. Brother Durkee has occupied a prominent position in the Central Association, serving as its corresponding secretary and on its board of trustees.

**Rev George Elliot**
Birth:
Mar. 1, 1757
Voluntown
New London County
Connecticut, USA
Death:
Mar. 30, 1817
Ames
Montgomery County
New York
Burial:
Ames Cemetery
Ames
Montgomery County, New York
Plot: Section 1

Rev. George Elliott was ordained Feb. 6, 1794, at the organization of the [Freewill Bapt] church in Florida, N.Y. of which he became pastor. He moved with the church to Bowman's Creek, now Ames, and remained its pastor until his death in 1817.

He was born in Pomfred, Conn, had been a teacher, and was wounded while in the Revolutionary army. His life was saved by the careful nursing of his betrothed, Miss Percy Kimball, who became his wife.

He was a tall, strong, man, intellectual, affectionate, unblamable, and, as a pastor, more than usually watchful. Hence, he had many warm friends, and exerted a very great influence for good.

He was converted at the age of fifteen and at twenty-four commenced preaching with the Open Communion Baptists at Richfield, N.Y. For twelve years he journeyed through the wilderness preaching two or three times a day, and his labors were blessed in the conversion of many souls." He died at the advanced age of 81 years.

**Rev Silvester R. Evans**
Birth:
Jul. 9, 1818
Livonia
Livingston County, New York
Death:
May 18, 1890
Burial:
Sugartown Cemetery
Sugartown
Cattaraugus County, New York

**John Farley**
Birth:
1777
New Hampshire
Death:
Dec. 12, 1858
Prospect, Oneida County,
New York
Burial:
Prospect Cemetery,
Prospect, Oneida County,
New York

**Rev William Fuller**
Birth:
1843
Death:
1908
Burial:
Garfield Cemetery
Stephentown
Rensselaer County, New York

Veteran of the Civil War Pastor 1876 - 1880 Free Baptist Church in Stephentown. Husband of Elizabeth Jane Sampson Fuller.

## James Salmon Gardner
Birth:
Jun. 24, 1822
New York
Death:
Apr. 23, 1881
Whitestown,
Oneida County, New York
Burial:
Grandview Cemetery,
Whitesboro,
Oneida County, New York

Prof. James Salmon Gardner graduated from Whitestown Seminary, N.Y. in 1846, and Hamilton College, Clinton, N.Y, in the class of 1849. In his studies he won the honors for superior scholarship and the degree of Doctor of Philosophy was bestowed by his Alma Mater in 1863. While in school he began teaching and in 1853 he became principal of Whitestown Seminary, a position which he held until his death. While head of the school, he devoted much attention to the successful pursuit of special studies in the sciences, and was interested in every movement for the advancement of education. The year of his graduation, 1849, he married Elizabeth E. PHILLIPS, sister of the Rev. Jeremiah Phillips, the missionary to India.

## Levi Geer Gardner
Birth:
1804
Massachusetts
Death:
Apr. 13, 1861
Burial:
Grandview Cemetery
Whitesboro
Oneida County, New York

His father served in the Revolution under Gen. Gates. In 1806 the family moved from Worthington, Mass., where Levi was born, to Plymouth, NY. Soon after this they with others united in forming a Free Baptist church under the labors of Elder Campbell. He was baptized by Eld. C. Easterbrooks and soon began to preach, receiving ordination in July 1825. Following the custom of that period, he went forth as an itinerant, preaching much on weekdays, as well as the Sabbath. He had great success in his extended work to the western part of the state and even into Canada. He baptized about 500 converts, nine churches were organized by his assistance, and his counsels were helpful to many, as he encouraged them to higher attainments and to more devoted living.

### Squire D. Gardner
Birth:
Feb. 1, 1808
Death:
May 18, 1864
Burial:
Grandview Cemetery,
Whitesboro,
Oneida County, New York

Squire D. was a brother of Rev. Levi Geer Gardner. His father did service in the Revolution under General Gates. He was an ordained Free Will Baptist minister, began preaching in 1841, at the Sherburne church, and was ordained about 1844. He was for seven years pastor of the church in Columbus, where many members were added and a house of worship erected. He was with the Plainfield church four years and saw refreshing seasons, and his labors with the Prospect church were greatly blessed. He was a judicious pastor, an instructive preacher, a candid and prudent councilor, and stood among his brethren in the front rank in the great moral conflict.

### Truman Gillett
Birth:
Jul. 23, 1779
Schuyler
Herkimer County, New York
Death:
Feb. 8, 1850
Burial:
Seventh Township Cemetery
Camden
Oneida County, New York

He was converted at 18 years of age. In 1809 he commenced preaching among the Methodists and after six years joined the Free Baptists in Russia, New York receiving his ordination on October 15, 1818. He labored much and had many conversions in Fairfield, Poland, and Oswego County, New York as well as in Canada..

## Waiting and watching within the gate.

Oakfield, Alabama, Claredon, Parma, and Middlebury churches.

In all these fields he was successful as the scores, if not hundreds, of converts testify.

He was stricken with apoplexy while in the pulpit at Ogden, whither he had gone from Parma to supply, and died aged 58 years. Nobly he accomplished life's great work, and died on the battle-field.

An ordained minister for 34 yrs to several churches in his area. He was a successful worker. He on two census' showed he was a FWB clergyman...I believe he was a man of intregity, as records attest.

## David Greene

Birth:
Oct. 1, 1807
Hoosick,
New York
Death:
Aug. 7, 1882
Fairport, New York
Burial:
Ouleout Cemetery
North Franklin
Delaware County,
New York

## Rev Hiram Gilman

Birth:
1810
Vermont
Death:
Jan. 23, 1868
New York
Burial:
North Byron Cemetery
Byron
Genesee County
New York

Rev. Hiram GILMAN, a native of Vermont, moved to New York in early life; was converted about 1831, and ordained by the Monroe Quarterly Meeting at Byron in 1834. The thirty-four years of his ministry were spent with the Ogden, Byron, Royalton, Ridgeway,

In his early life he was a resident of Delaware County and with his wife in 1836 joined the Franklin church that had been recently organized. Two years later he was chosen Deacon and in 1842 was ordained as it's pastor, a relationship he continued for 18 years adding to the church by baptisms.

**Rev Ansel Griffith**
Birth:
Feb. 10, 1804
Herkimer County
New York
Death:
May 15, 1892
Clymer
Chautauqua County
New York
Burial:
Town Line Cemetery
Cassadaga
Chautauqua County
New York

Rev. Ansel Griffith, was ordained June 24, 1832, age 28yrs. A Freewill Baptist minister for 60 years. He was converted five years before, and preached while teaching and while a student at Hamilton, N.Y. He engaged with success in revival work before ordination, and afterward ministered in the Schroeppel, Scriba, and Phoenix churches.

In 1846, after being laid aside by disease for a year, he continued his work at Clayton, Theresa, Lyme, Three-Mile Bay, Harrisburgh, and Turin. He was pastor of the Townline Baptist Church for many years. He was a successful minister and baptized over two hundred converts. His spouse was Nancy S.Griffith in 1850 census and forward. (The 1870 census, listed spouse as "Sophia" which was probably Nancy's middle name, as "Nancy" was spouse in 1880.) Year of their marriage is unk at this time.

Inscription:
"Blessed are the dead which die in the Lord"

**Rev Susan Cilley Griffin**
Birth:
Feb. 28, 1851
Boston
Houghton County,Michigan
Death:
Jan. 5, 1927
New York

Burial:
Keuka Park Cemetery
Jerusalem
Yates County,New York

Rev. Susan "Libbie" (Cilley) Griffin was the daughter of E. G. Cilley. She was the 2nd wife of Rev. Dr. Zebina Flavious Griffin. They were married Jackson, Michigan February 28, 1881. She was a Free Baptist Missionary to India 1873-1909, a teacher, and studied one year at Woman's Medical College at New York, and then entered again upon her course of study at Hillsdale. She did effective work organizing women to raise mission's funds for India.

**Rev Zebina Flavious Griffin**
Birth:
Nov. 14, 1844
Byron
Ogle County,Illinois
Death:
Feb. 11, 1938
Keuka Park

Yates County, New York
Burial:
Keuka Park Cemetery
Jerusalem
Yates County, New York

Rev. Dr. Zebina Flavious Griffin was the son of Rev. Jacob and Emmaline (Wade) Griffin. Mary Gertrude (Harwood) Griffin was his 1st wife. They were married July 20, 1865 and she died November 18, 1879. Rev. Susan "Libbie" (Cilley) Griffin was his 2nd wife. They were married February 28, 1881 and she died January 5, 1927. He was graduated from Hillsdale College, Mich. 1881, where his first wife, Mary Harwood, died in 1879; He and 2nd wife Libbie Cilley, served missionaries to India; he also had a successful pastorate at Gilbert's Mills, NY.

Alma Harriet (Goulton) Bond Griffin was his 3rd wife. They were married in 1934 when he was 85 years old. He was a minister in the Baptist Church and a missionary to India 1883-1909.

### C. E. Hallock
Birth:
July 31, 1847
Constantia, New York
Death:
May 6, 1895
Burial:
Constantia Center Cemetery
Constantia Center
Oswego County, New York

He experienced religion in 1869 and was ordained June 2, 1878 after which he served the Constantia church as pastor. He was actively connected with the temperance work for 18 years.

### Ely Hannibal
Birth:
Mar. 18, 1780
Fairfield,
Fairfield County, Connecticut
Death:
Aug. 28, 1876
Clarkson,
Monroe County, New York
Burial:
Garland Cemetery, Clarkson,
Monroe County, New York,
Plot: 1 - 8

Freewill Baptist pioneer minister in New York. Rev. Ely was converted Aug. 1806, and two yrs after, he joined a Baptist church; and removing to Yates (later Clarkson), NY, in 1811, he assisted in organizing the church in Sweden. In 1820 he joined a Free Baptist church that was organized in Clarkson; and the church had a council to ordain him on June 12, 1824. A revival immediately began,

and fifty were converted. He preached in the surrounding towns and soon became a leader among the people in the rude dwellings of those times, in the big schoolhouses, and in the church, then uncommon, he preached with great earnestness the free gospel of Jesus Christ. There was scarcely a church organized w/o his aid, or a minister ordained without his counsel. He was not a scholar in any modern sense, but was at once popular and successful.

Rev. Joseph Hallenbeck died at his residence in Corning, Dec. 20, aged fifty-nine years. He had been a resident for about thirty five years. He was a native of Schoharie Co. He was by trade a stone mason, and followed that vocation till disabled by illness. He was enterprising, and built several brick buildings for business purposes, all of which he sold except that leased to C. W. Smith. He a contractor, he was faithful to his obligations, and as an employer he was kind, considerate and honorable. He was highly esteemed by those with whom he had business dealings or relations, and maintained a reputation for honesty, and the sure fulfillment of his word. He was for many years a zealous Christian, and a preacher, first of the Free Methodist, and after that of the Free Baptist Church. He was the pastor of the Free Baptist Church in Corning, and owned the meeting house, which a year ago at much expense, the most of it his own, he fitted up so that it could be used for Gospel Temperance meetings; and he was always enthusiastic on the subject of Temperance, or of religion. He preached every winter in some remote and sparsely settled locality, and his whole compensation for a score of years for these services would not pay for the expense of his horse and conveyance. He thus labored on Handy Creek, in Southport, Kelly town, in Caton, and Curtis Hollow, in Campbell. Successful revivals there and in Knoxville, in this town, repeatedly occurred under his preaching, and he claimed that the converts "held out" well in all of his fields of labor. In his early life he was for some years a sailor. He had no educational advantages but that did not deter him from preaching as he had opportunity; and no inclemency of the weather, roughness of the roads, or fatigue of the service after laboring at his trade, for a week, prevent him from meeting at his appointments. His services were largely attended on Sunday afternoon at the Free Baptist Church.

### Joseph Hallenbeck

Birth:
1820
Death:
Dec. 20, 1878
Burial:
Hope Cemetery
Corning
Steuben County
New York

Rev. Joseph Hallenbeck died at his residence in Corning, N.Y., Dec. 20, 1878, age 59 years. He had lived there thirty-five years and with Elder Rollins, organized the Corning Church. His preaching was with fervor, and evidenced familiarity with the Bible.

### Luther Hanson

Birth:
1820
Death:
1894
Burial:
Glenview Cemetery
Pulteney
Steuben County, New York,

He was licensed in 1845 and attended Whitestown Seminary between the years of 1846-47. His ordination took place June, 1849. His pastorates were in Maine and New York and he had several revivals under his labors. Besides his preaching, he was engaged for several years in teaching. In 1853 he was a delegate to the General Conference.

### Isaac Hill

Birth:
1783
Death:
1840
Burial:
West Hill Cemetery
Hornby
Steuben County, New York

He was converted in his youth and ordained on February 22, 1838 and died at the age of 57 years. He was earnest and pointed in preaching, gentleman in manner, and much respected.

### Rev James Wightman Hills

Birth:
Oct. 1, 1816
Fabius
Onondaga County
New York, USA
Death:
May 5, 1898
New York
Burial:
Quaker Basin Cemetery

DeRuyter
Madison County
New York

Rev. James Wightman HILLS, granadson of Elder Jno. HILLS of the Six Principle Baptists and older brother of Rev. O.C. HILLS, was born at Fabius, NY, Oct 1, 1816. He was educated at Fabius' Academy, De Ruyter Institute and Whitestown Seminary, all in NY., and received license to preach in 1836, and was ordained by the Spafford Quarterly Meeting (QM) Sept. 8, 1844. His pastorates have been Willet, Sherburne, Virgil, and dryden, Willet (again), and Union Center, NY; Jackson and West Lennox, PA; Summer Hill, Philadelphia, Depauville, Holmsville, and Oxford, NY; East Troy and sullivan, PA, Caroline and Dryden, NY, Warren Center, Windham and Belle Vernon, PA; South Plymouth, Prospect, and Grant, NY.

The years of his long ministry have been filled with active service, some of the time two or more churches being under his care. He has engaged in many revivals and organized seven churches. In the time of the war he labored in the South under the Christian Commission.

He was for several years clerk and treasurer of the Susquehanna Yearly Meeting, and has twice served as delegate to the General Conference.

He was married to Miss Clarissa Quivey in 1847, and two years after her death to Miss Rebecca A.

Randall in 1862. Both were of Cincinnatus, NY, the latter a teacher in the academy at that place.

### Charles H Hoag
Birth:
March 25, 1835
Ridgeway, New York
Death:
Dec. 16, 1904
Burial:
Evergreen Cemetery
Pine Plains
Dutchess County, New York

He turned to God when he was 18 years of age and married Mrs. Minerva Power on December 25, 1858. He received his license to preach in 1876 and was ordained on December 11, 1880. His ministry it was in the Genesee Yearly Meeting most all of his ministry. --Pine Plains Register, 23 Dec 1904.

### Isaac J Hoag
Birth:
Mar. 11, 1819
Chatham, New York
Death:
Mar. 22, 1891
New York
Burial:
Union Cemetery
North Creek
Warren County, New York

Converted at age 15 and became acquainted with the Free Baptists and united with them at West Stephentown. He received license to preach from the Rensselaer Quarterly Meeting in 1846 and supplied two churches for two years in that area. He was ordained on September 10, 1848 where he served pastorates in New York and Massachusetts. He assisted in organizing four churches and baptized nearly 400 converts.

### Ephraim Chapelle Hodge
Birth:
Jan. 17, 1876
New York, USA
Death:
Mar. 22, 1941
Jefferson County, New York
Burial:
Adams Rural Cemetery
Adams
Jefferson County, New York

He was ordained at Oneonta Plains in September, 1850 and preached in the churches of the Otsego Quarterly Meeting having ministered the West Onenota church 20 years and for shorter periods other churches in the area. He was held in high esteem by the people of whom he lived around so long. He baptized about 500 converts.

### Rev George R Holt
Birth:
Apr. 26, 1844
Lykens
Crawford County
Ohio
Death:
Aug. 18, 1931
Hilton
Monroe County
New York
Burial:
Parma Union Cemetery
Parma
Monroe County
New York
Plot: Sec. 9, West Div, Lot 7

His parents were Martin W. and Salley L (Black) HOLT. He was educated at Hillsdale College, Mich., in the college and theological departments. Devoting his life to God in September, 1854, he received license to preach in 1865, and was ordained Feb. 24, 1868. While pursuing his studies at Hillsdale, he had the pastoral care of the Cook's Prairie church three years and of the Pittsford church three years and of the Pittsford church two years. He has since done substantial work as pastor of the Rome and Cambridge churches seven years, and of the Jackson church eight years. He has conducted several series of revival meetings, organized one church and baptized 209 converts. For six years he served on the executive board of the Home Mission Society, and he was a trustee of Hillsdale College. He was a representative of the Michigan Yearly Meeting in the General Conference. He was married July, 1868, to Marilla Waller. In 1888 he became pastor at North Parma, NY, After his wife, Marilla, died he married Annette M Woodruff, abt 1897.

He was a Corporal in Co. D, 12th Wisconsin Inf.Enlisted Sept 1861, W.Bend, WI, and Disch'd, Dec. 13, 1864. (He is listed in the Parmar Union Cemetery list of Veterans.)

### Solomon Howe

Birth:
Nov. 4, 1786
Hillsborough County,
New Hampshire
Death:
May 9, 1859
Smyrna
Chenango County, New York
Burial:
Cincinnatus Cemetery
Cincinnatus
Cortland County, New York

He was converted in 1804, licensed in 1812 and ordained in New Hampshire in 1819. He labored in New Hampshire and Vermont until 1826, when he moved to New York and became one of the honored fathers of the Union Quarterly Meeting. He spent many years in the MacDonough Quarter Meeting and from 1845 to 1850 was in the Nelson Quarterly Meeting.

### Daniel Huling
Birth:
May 5, 1797
Washington County,
Rhode Island
Death:
Jan. 8, 1853
French Creek,
Chautauqua County,
New York
Burial:
Cutting Cemetery
Cutting
Chautauqua County, New York

He was converted in 1817 and ordained in 1847.

### Robert Hunt
Birth:
Nov. 25, 1792
Schoharie County, New York
Death:
Dec. 7, 1872
Utica
Oneida County, New York
Burial:
Forest Hill Cemetery
Utica
Oneida County, New York
Plot: 30B-1 (Lot 1285)

He was a younger brother of William Hunt and received ordination among the Free Communion Baptists of New York about 1835. He was a man of considerable education, progressive in his tendencies and a good pastor.

### Rogers Ide

Birth:
May, 1788
Vermont,
Death:
Jun. 2, 1863
Spafford
Onondaga County, New York
Burial:
Borodino Cemetery
Borodino, Onondaga County,
New York

Ide fought in the War of 1812, and co-founded the Free Will Baptist Church in Spafford, NY. In 1831 he began preaching, and by 1836 was ordained. Shortly thereafter, he traveled to the southern part of Indiana, where he preached against the sins of slavery, even when slave owners had a reward on his head.

### Chester H Jackson

Birth:
Oct. 21, 1834
Death:
Dec. 9, 1912
Burial:
Alger Cemetery
Hume
Allegany County,
New York

He was converted in 1849; was a student at Pike Seminary, New York in 1860-61, and received ordination June 7, 1863. He went from Pike, New York to Michigan where he ministered to the Dover Church while pursuing theological studies at Hillsdale College.

### Daniel Jackson

Birth:
Apr. 12, 1804
Death:
Dec. 9, 1890
Burial:
Varysburg Cemetery, Varysburg,
Wyoming County, New York

A leading Free Will Baptist minister in New England who was born in Madison, New Hampshire. He received his early religious impressions from Rev. John Colby, and was converted under the labors of Rev. Jonathan Woodman in 1818. He was ordained at East Ossipee, New Hampshire on Sept. 14, 1826. His pastorates were: E. Ossipee (five years), Wheelock, VT (two yrs), Topsham (four yrs), Meredith Village, N.H., Lewiston Falls, ME, Charleston, Mass, Topsham, ME, Saco, South Berwick, Lyndon Centre, VT. and Gardiner City, ME. After 1854, he traveled in the South, and returning, became pastor at Wells, ME. In these pastorates he was successful. At Topsham as a result of one revival ninety-six were baptized. He was active in the general denominational work, having served in the General Conferences of 1827, 1841, and 1880, the centennial meeting.

He was married to Miss Mary P. Kenneson, Sept. 20, 1827, and after her death, to Miss Hannah B. Fernald in 1853, and again bereaved, to Mrs. Clara Hewes, in 1857, with whom, after a long life of usefulness he is passing the remaining years at Varysburgh, N.Y. He wrote An Autobiography of 214 pages in 1859.

**Nelson A Jackson**
Birth:
Dec. 28, 1811
Arcade, N. Y
Death:
Aug. 30, 1871
New Hudson, N. Y
Burial:
Arcade Rural Cemetery
Arcade, Wyoming County,
New York

Jackson was born of Quaker ancestry died at aged 59 years. He was converted under the labors of Elder H. Jenkins when nineteen years of age, and licensed to preach five years later. After spending some time in study, he was ordained in his native town June 6, 1841. His pastorates were with the Varysburgh, Arcade, Elton, Yorkshire, Ashford, and Humphrey and Great Valley churches. But one testimony was borne of him: that he was an earnest, loving, Christian minister. His quiet manner helped to develop thoughtful, abiding piety.

### Calvin Jenkins
Birth:
Jan. 18, 1798
Stoddard, Cheshire,
New Hampshire
Death:
Jan. 31, 1882
Burial:
St. Lawrence County,
New York

---

### Nathaniel Ketchum
Birth:
Unknown
Death:
Jan. 11, 1838
Burial:
Pike Cemetery, Pike
Wyoming County, New York

He was ordained in 1813 and labored in New York. In 1816 he joined the Bethany Quarterly Meeting and leader in the Erie Quarterly Meeting which was sustained by a very strong revival under his labors.

### George Washington Knapp
Birth:
Sep. 23, 1842
Cameron
Steuben County
New York
Death:
Jun. 20, 1892
New York
Burial:
South Hill Cemetery
Cameron
Steuben County
New York

Rev. George W. Knapp, was the son of William and Eliza J. (Osborn) KNAPP. He professed faith in 1851, and received license to preach in 1862, and ordained a Freewill Baptist minister in 1866. He pastored in Meredith Centre, and Contoocook, NH; Granville NY; and Aurora and Kenesaw, Neb. He was blessed in his ministry with over one hundred conversions in one year. In 1883, he was elected delegate to the General

Conference. He was educated in Hillsdale College, Mich, and Bates Theological School in Lewiston, Maine. In Sept. 1865, he married Caroline [Carrie] Dennis.

---

**Rev Stephen Krum**
Birth:
1807
Death:
Feb. 13, 1903
Burial:
Snyder Hill Cemetery
Dryden
Tompkins County
New York,

Pastor of the Snyder Hill Free Will Baptist Church
Husband of Almira Coon
Parents: Mathew Krum & Margaret VanDermark

---

Rev John M. Langworthy
Birth:
Mar. 6, 1831
New York
Death:
Aug. 17, 1896
New York
Burial:
New Forest Cemetery
Utica
Oneida County
New York

An ordained FWB minister and pastor. His father, Nathan, was also active in the church as was his bro, Nathan, Jr.

James Letts
Birth:
Unknown
Death:
Dec. 9, 1864
Burial:
Pleasant Lawn Cemetery
Paris, Oswego County, New York

Letts, a native of Ulster, N. Y., was converted in 1850 and united with the Paris church at its organization. He acted as colporteur and agent of the American Tract Society three years, during which time he also held revival services and was connected with the Parish, Lyndon, and Angelica churches. Early in 1858 he held services with the Burns church; many were added and he became its pastor. He was ordained March 3, 1861, and in 1863 returned to the Oswego Q. M., and took charge of the Parish, Redfield, and Constantia churches, holding revivals with them and with the Osceola church the following winter. He was an active, persevering, and successful minister, and died of fever at 40 years of age. The minutes of the national Association of the Randall movement of Free Will Baptists said his death was 1864.

---

## Waiting and watching within the gate.

---

### W. A. Lighthall
Birth:
Aug. 22, 1813
Fort Ann,
Washington County, New York
Death:
Jul. 8, 1865
Burial:
Pike Cemetery,
Pike,
Wyoming County, New York

In May 1832, he moved to Weathersfield, and in September became totally blind. But this providence brought to him spiritual light. He was baptized in 1835 and licensed to preach in October, 1837.

Immediately commenced to preach at Middlebury, and in four years the church increased greatly in strength and numbers. At Attica he labored with good success three years. Having thus given proof of his call to the ministry, he was ordained a Freewill Baptist minister at Varysburgh in May, 1845. His later labors were with the churches in Weathersfield, Hamburg, Cowlesville, Ellington, Chautaqua, and Pomfret, besides itinerant preaching. His mind was vigorous and clear; his memory, quickened by loss of sight; was retentive, and his powers were devoted fully to his work

### Rev Aaron B. Loomis
Birth:
Sep. 13, 1837
Lexington
Greene County
New York
Death:
Jun. 27, 1927
New York
Burial:
Forest Park Cemetery
Camden
Oneida County
New York

An ordined Freewill Baptist minister in NY, after he had served NY military in the Civil War. He was a dedicated minister.

### Horatio N. Loring
**Birth:**
1806
Death:
1847
Burial:
Forest Hill Cemetery
UticaOneida County
New York

He was ordained in Rhode Island in 1825. He was one of the four young man, under 30 years of age, who sat in the first General Conference with Rev. Zalmon Tobey. He was delegate to the fourth General Conference in 1830, and Sec. of the sixth General Conference at Meredith, New Hampshire in 1832. He was pastor of the Broad St. Baptist
Church.
Source: Forest Hill burial list carried in the *Utica Morning Herald and Daily Gazette*, May 30 1882.

### Rev Arad Losee
Birth:
Jan. 11, 1821
Corinth
Saratoga County
New York

Death:
Mar. 23, 1897
Burial:
Sherman Cemetery
Sherman
Chautauqua County
New York

Rev. Arad Loosee (sic), of Sherman, NY, son of John and Lucy (Ellis) Loosee was brought into the Lord's service in 1834, studied at Edon Academy, Erie Co., and began to preach in 1849. He was ordained in June 1853, by a council from the French Creek Q.M., Rev. B. McKoon, preaching the sermon. His ministry was in western NY, and Penn, his pastorates being Lake Pleasant, Waterford, Rockdale, Salem, Greenwood, Spring Creek, Bloomfield, Greenfield and Northeast, PA, and Charlotte, Sherman, Collins, South Harmony, and Clymer and Harmonny NY, frequently having the care of two churches at a time. He has baptized about four hundred converts, and served the Yearly Meeting as delegate to the General Conference.

### John H. Loveless
Birth:
1809
Death:
Aug. 22, 1871
Johnsburgh, N. Y.
Burial:
Lynwood Church Cemetery
Hadley, Saratoga County,
New York

Loveless died at age 61 years. He was born in Poultney, Vt., and when seventeen years of age united with the Free Communion Baptists in Hadley, N. Y. The following year he began to preach and, being ordained in 1842, continued his labor at Hadley with unremitting ardor. He also labored in Poestenkill, N. Y., and six years in the Monroe Q. M., returning to his former home for the closing years of service. He was an amiable, modest pastor, faithful in precept and example, and his ministry was crowned with success.

### Daniel Lyon
Birth:
Unknown
Death:
Sep. 23, 1842
Walworth, New York
Burial:
Walworth Center Cemetery
Wayne County, New York

He died at age 47. In 1824 he was ordained and became pastor of the Walworth Church having been a member since its organization in 1816. He was a successful preacher, a wise counselor, a father to his church. More than 300 converts were baptized by him and his death was greatly lamented.

### Enoch Mack
Birth:
Jan. 30, 1806
Connecticut
Death:
Feb. 20, 1881
Catskill
Greene County, New York
Burial:
Catskill Village Cemetery
Catskill
Greene County, New York

Rev. Enoch Mack, M.D., born in Connecticut, in his childhood with his family moved to Susquehanna Co. PA, and here, after graduating in medicine he practiced his profession. After a time, he turned toward the ministry and became interested in temperance and anti-slavery causes. In 1833, he went on horseback to Philadelphia, where, with Garrison, Whittier, and others, he signed the Declaration of Sentiments, put forth by the Anti-Slavery Society.

He was attracted to the Free Baptists because of their anti-slavery sentiments, and became an early contributor to the "Morning Star". At the suggestion of Editor William Burr, he was called to Dover. NH, in 1835, and ordained pastor of the first Free Baptist church there. Subsequently, he resigned the pastorate to serve as agent of the Foreign Mission Board, and was also corresponding secretary of the Foreign and Home Mission Societies. During these years and later, he was a frequent correspondent and an editorial contributor of the "Star," and his vigorous pen did much to awaken an interest in missionary work and in the other great moral and Christian enterprises of the day. About 1849, he went to New York City, where he was appointed city missionary for the northern portion of the city. In this capacity he served with earnestness and devotion nineteen years. His last years were spent with his son at Catskill Station in Columbia County.His devoted labors for those causes that would save men from intemperance, give freedom to the bondmen, rescue the heathen millions from idolatry, and lift up the degraded in our great cities, evince the breadth of his sympathies and give him a high place among the benefactors of our race. He was married to Phebe L. Roberts, and they were on 1850 census together, along with Narcissa, a daughter, age 17.On the 1860 census, Enoch stated he was a 'retired minister.'

---

**William Mack**
Birth:
1798
Lyme
New London County, Connecticut
Death:
1877
Steuben County, New York
Burial:
Mack Cemetery
Steuben County, New York

He was an active preacher for forty-five years. His labors were mostly in northern Pennsylvania and southern New York, where his ministry was abundantly blessed in the salvation of souls. He assisted in organizing most of the churches of the Tuscarora quarterly meeting. He was the son of Samuel and Mary Mack, Husband of Eliza Kimball. Mack Cemetery is a family cemetery that contains six graves and is located on Mack Road.

**Benjamin McKoon**
Birth:
Sep. 2, 1799
Death:
Nov. 16, 1880
Columbia, N. Y.,
Burial:
Millers Mills Cemetery
Millers Mills,
Herkimer County,
New York

Rev. Benjamin, a brother of Rev. D. W. McKoon, died aged 81 years. At the age of seventeen, he obeyed the call to a Christian life and was baptized by Rev. Wm. Hunt. He was ordained at Unadilla Forks in 1823, and for fifty-seven years, he preached the gospel with zeal and earnestness, and often with great power. His early labors were in the Chemung Valley and adjacent country. Afterwards for sixteen years he labored in central New York and in Oswego and Jefferson counties, his efforts being crowned with very marked success. Then, after years of successful ministry in western New York, he moved from Ellington to Hillsdale to educate his children. Returning in 1861, he preached at Columbia, German Flatts, Oxford and Holmesville, and, six years later, took up pastoral work in Chautauqua and Cattaraugus Counties, and continued it until health would no longer permit.

He had baptized about eight hundred converts, and the last three years of life were largely spent in visiting former fields of labor, confirming the saints. Christ and his cross were themes he loved to dwell upon, and the atonement was to him the pivotal point on which rested the great work of the soul's salvation. He was a delegate to the General Conference of 1847 from the Holland Purchase Y. M. His son, Prof. Bela P. McKoon, of Hillsdale College, Whitestown Seminary, and later of Cornell

University, in these institutions rendered efficient service as an educator.

### Daniel W McKoon
Birth:
Jun. 6, 1811
Herkimer County, New York
Death:
Jan. 4, 1871
Sugartown
Cattaraugus County, New York
Burial:
Sugartown Cemetery
Sugartown
Cattaraugus County, New York

Rev. Daniel William McKoon, a native of Columbia, N.Y., was baptized by Rev. Wm. Hunt when eighteen year of age. He was licensed to preach in 1838 and ordained Feb. 9, 1840 in Free Baptist Church. He commenced immediately a six-year' pastorate with the Newport and Poland church, sixty being added to the church by baptism and lasting good resulted. In 1847 he was prostrated by disease, which so affected the mind that on recovery he found it necessary to study the alphabet again and regain his former knowledge step by step. After this, twenty years of usefulness remained to him, which were spent in the Cattaraugus and Chautauqua Quarterly Meetings, his last pastorate being with the Ashford church. He died at Orlean aged 59 years. Brother McKoon was a warm-hearted Christian, earnest in every good work and faithful to duty. As a preacher he was systematic and pathetic. In his early ministry he rendered efficient service in securing friends and funds for Whitestown Seminary at a time when both were needed. He represented the Central N.Y. Yearly Meeting in the General Conference of 1844. His son, Newton C. McKoon of Ellicottsville, N.Y., was for many years clerk of the Cattaraugus Q.M., and commissioner of schools for Cattaraugus County.

### Newton C McKoon
Birth:
Dec. 17, 1835
Herkimer
Herkimer County, New York
Death:
Aug. 27, 1906
Humphrey
Cattaraugus County,
New York
Burial:
Sugartown Cemetery
Sugartown
Cattaraugus County,
New York

His parents were Rev. Daniel W. McKoon and Jane T. (Young) McKoon.There is an enlistment for him in the Civil War Muster, of 1862, Great Valley, NY. He became a Free Baptist minister and was a leader in the Humphrey Free Bapt Church, where his father ministered. He was also clerk of the Yearly meeting for many years, and was Commissioner of schools.He married Ann Crary (1845-1914), in 1865 per 1900 census.

### Rev Melville Corner Miner
Birth:
Jan. 18, 1857
Death:
Feb. 17, 1923
Burial:
West Oneonta Cemetery
Oneonta
Otsego County
New York
Plot: BR-05

Rev. Dr. Miner was ordained to preach Dec. 16, 1883, and held pastorates in Indiana and Osseo, Michigan. Supporting himself as teacher and pastor he has attended Ridgeville College, Indiana, and Hillsdale College, Theology Dept. 1885-1888. Ordained Freewill Baptist minister; DD probably conferred by Hillsdale College in Mich, late 1880's.

He married Anna R. Root, May 25, 1873.

### Robert Edward Nesbitt
Birth:
Nov. 19, 1854
Hamlin, NY
Death:
Oct. 12, 1893
Burial:
Blossom Cemetery
Hamlin
Monroe County
New York

Born in Hamlin, NY. Son of James and Isabella "Gabe" (Edgeworth) Nesbit, who came to the United States from Co Cavan, Ireland in 1850. Married Emma Stuart of Hamlin on Nov. 29, 1882. Father of: Stuart James (1885-1959), William Henry Francis (1887-1964), who became Secretary General of General Electric in Canada, and Nellie Mae (Walter) Blodgett (1890-1965). Attended Brockport Normal

School and taught in the Hamlin School district. Went to Seminary at Hillsdale College (Michigan) and then returned to become a well-known temperance minister in the Free Will Baptist Church. Served as minister at Walker, Scriba, and Hilton, NY churches.

Was also well known as a carpenter. Died in Hamlin, NY at age 39. Was originally buried at High Street Cemetery in Brockport, NY. Body moved to Blossom Cemetery when his wife Emma died in 1907.

**Rev Samuel Newell**
Birth: 1788
Barnstead,
New York
Death: Sep. 6, 1880
Lawrence
Nassau County
New York
Burial:
Mound Hill Cemetery
Nicholville
St. Lawrence County

New York, Plot: 290-7A

He served in the Legislature from Woodstock and was converted in 1831, at Johnstown, Canada, where he began to preach with the Methodists. In 1837 he settled in Lawrence, NY where he joined the Free Baptists. His ministry was mostly confined to the Lawrence, Hopkinton and Dickinson churches. He was a logical and instructive preacher, and a most exemplary christian; and even after he had passed his fourscore years, he was listened to with interest.

An ordained Free Baptist minister, died aged 91 yrs. Spouse was Polly Erwin.

**Asahel Nichols**
Birth:
1851
Ames, New York
Death:
unknown
Burial:
Ames Cemetery
Ames
Montgomery County,
New York

He joined the church in his native town, Chesterfield, Massachusetts, in 1840. He later taught two terms at Geauga Seminary, Ohio and graduated from the theological department of Oberlin College, Oberlin, Ohio in 1846. He returned then to preach in Maine and New York.

### John Nicholson
Birth:
Mar. 21, 1793
Connecticut
Death:
Apr. 7, 1863
Burial:
Steere Cemetery
East McDonough,
Chenango County,
New York

Nicholson was a native of Stonington, Conn., was converted and united with the McDonough, N. Y., church in 1813. He was ordained at the session of the Q. M. held at Plymouth, N. Y., in June, 1833, and continued with the McDonough church, except two years with the Second Otselic and three with the German, 1854-59, until his death, which occurred at the advanced age of 70 years. his wife was the Roby Steere (1798 - 1840).

### William Nutting
Birth:
Nov. 6, 1794
Death:
Jan. 25, 1872
Parish, N. Y,
Burial:
Nutting Cemetery
West Monroe, Oswego County,
New York

At the age of twenty-five, after many conflicts, he consecrated himself to the Master's service. His ministry, for nearly forty-five years, was mostly with the churches of the Oswego Q. M. He was an eccentric, zealous man, useful in the work of the Lord. At his death one son was state senator in Virginia and another district attorney of Oswego County, New York.

**Thomas Parker**
Birth:
1794
Foster, R.I.
Death:
Aug. 4, 1865
Perrinton (Fairport), N. Y.,
Burial:
Elmwood Cemetery
Perrinton,
Monroe County, New York

He was converted under the labors of Rev. J. Fowler and joined the Walworth church. At the age of twenty-eight he commenced preaching in Penfield, and soon a church was organized there. He was ordained in 1828 and remained pastor of the church twenty-eight years. He also preached in Ontario, Webster, Macedon and Perrinton. For some years before his death he did not have the care of a church, but preached as opportunity presented. During his ministry he baptized over five hundred converts, married 500 couples and attended more than one thousand funerals. His joy was in the Lord, both in life and at its close.

**Rev Washington Parker**
Birth:
Aug. 7, 1829
Chautauqua County
New York
Death:
Jun. 19, 1901
Burial:
Sherman Cemetery, Sherman
Chautauqua County,New York

His parents were George and Myra (Gardinier) PARKER. He Married Sarah L. Goodrich in 1852, and ordained a Free Baptist minister June 7, 1868.
He pastored twelve years with Waterford and Lake Pleasant churches in Pennsylvania. He also served Wellsburg and Bloomfield churches in PA. He then was with the church at Sherman, NY. In all these pastorates his work was successful and blessed.

### A. P. Phinney
Birth:
Apr. 8, 1828
Reading, New York
Death:
Nov. 7, 1897
Burial:
Pleasant Lawn Cemetery
Parish
Oswego County, New York

He experienced religion in 1857 in Alleghany County. The same year he was licensed to preach and supplied churches near his home for about three years where his labors were blessed. He moved to Oswego County in 1864 and was ordained on June 10, 1867 under the ministry of the First Parish Church which was greatly strengthened and the Second Parish Church was organized. In 1870 became the pastor of the Hastings church.

### Rev Thomas Pratt
Birth:
1747
Madison County
New York
Death:
1822
Rushford
Allegany County
New York
Burial:
First Burying Ground Cemetery
Rushford
Allegany County, New York

Rev. Thomas Pratt, a native of Middlebury, Massachusetts, moved to Rushford, NY in 1812, where he remained until his death at the age of 73 years. He was converted in 1822, he was united with the Rushford & Lyndon churches & soon felt called to preach. He was ordained about 1836*, having been licensed some years before, and some of the time had care of several churches. he was a man of power, outspoken & positive & represented his Yearly Meeting in the General Conference of Freewill Baptist" *Ordained, Nov. 18, 1834.

A History of Rushford, shows that they had a semi- centennial celebration in 1859, in which " Rev. Thomas L Pratt, delivered an introductory speech, which was highly praised by all there."[ the author stated it was a shame it couldn't have been preserved.}

### Rev Levi C. Preston
Birth:
Nov. 10, 1829
Death:
Aug. 8, 1878
Caroline Center
Tompkins County
New York
Burial:
Caroline Centre Cemetery
Caroline Center
Tompkins County
New York

### Thomas L Pratt
Birth:
May 6, 1794
Madison County
New York
Death:
Jun. 9, 1873
Rushford
Allegany County,
New York
Burial:
Rushford Cemetery
Rushford
Allegany County,
New York

Rev. Thomas L. Pratt, was a pioneer minister in Allegany Co. NY. He was ordained Nov. 18, 1834, and ministered to churches in that area until he died.

He was ordained in 1858, and after four years' active work, failing health compelled him to change his work and residence. He moved to Centralia, Kan., where he exerted an influence by his modesty, charity and general benevolence. Nearing the end of life with consumption, he returned to New York to die. For the purpose of educating his children he made his home at Hillsdale, Mich., several years

**Charles Putnam**
Birth:
Unknown
Death:
Feb. 1, 1878
Byron, N. Y.
Burial:
West Bethany Cemetery
West Bethany, Genesee County,
New York

Putnam was a native of Bethany, died at aged 55 years. After graduating from Union College in 1848, he engaged in teaching at Varysburgh, N. Y. He was converted under the labors of Rev. M. H. Abbey, and after a few months was ordained. After teaching and preaching at Cowlesville, when Pike Seminary was purchased he became its principal, and served the church as pastor. Here his labors were severe and exhaustive, but crowned with generouis results. Most of his labors were in western New York,

his last pastorate being at Byron. He was an excellent minister, in preaching logical, instructive and inspiring, and frequent revivals were enjoyed.

**Rev Thomas R Reed**
Birth:
Oct. 13, 1830
Lowville
Lewis County, New York
Death:
Mar. 23, 1894
Burial:
Seventh-Day Baptists Settlement
Cemetery
Watson
Lewis County, New York

Rev. Thomas R. Reed, of Petrie's Corners, N.Y., is son of William and Chloe (Wetmore) Reed. He was brought to Christ in 1850 and, three years later, was married to Martha A. Robinson. He received license to preach in 1865, and was ordained in 1868 by the Seventh

Day Baptist church of Watson, of which he has continued pastor. Some ten years since he began also to minister to the New Bremen and Watson church, which about 1865 became connected with the Jefferson Quarterly Meeting, of the St. Lawrence Yearly Meeting.

### Richard Richardson
Birth:
Jan. 14, 1799
Leek
Staffordshire, England
Death:
Jun. 10, 1872
Varysburg
Wyoming County, New York
Burial:
Cowlesville Cemetery
Cowlesville
Wyoming County, New York

He was a student at the Montpelier and Bates College. He was converted in 1876 and was licensed on June 28, 1885, and ordained July 10, 1887. He also was a student at Cobbett divinity school. He married Elizabeth about 1822 and after her death, he married Sally Munger about 1845

### Edson M. Roel
Birth:
December 28, 1858
Dummerston,
Vermont
Death:
1939
Burial:
Morningside Cemetery
Hartford
Washington County,
New York

On March 1, 1882, he was married to Etta L. Payne. Having given himself to God in the work of the gospel ministry, he was licensed in 1879, and ordained in 1884. He is held pastors in Vermont and New York.

### Rev D M Lafayette Rollin

Birth:
Aug. 12, 1804
Franklin County
Maine
Death:
1895
Maine
Burial:
Maple Wood Cemetery
Boston
Erie County
New York

He was the son of Samuel Rollin and Susan (Lawrence) Rollin. (Some genealogies give his first name as De Marquis Lafayette). His land records show "D.M. Lafayette Rollin." On August 29, 1837, he married Miss Mary Carey, in Boston, NY. She was the eldest daughter of the Hon. Truman Carey of Boston. There are four children recorded in censuses: Mary; Delia; Carey; and Emma.

Rev. D.M.L. Rollin, was taught early in life to love books. He received his formal training at Farmington Seminary, under the Principal of the Seminary, Nathaniel Green, A.M. In 1825, his views and feelings changed, and he publicly professed the Christian religion and united with the Free Baptist Church.

In 1829, he was ordained by a council called by the church. He turned his attention to the study of theology and began upon a successful work in the Wayne Quarterly Meeting which soon became the Ohio and Pennsylvania Yearly Meeting subsequently, he labored in western New York. In this state he held pastorates with many of the strongest churches and exerted an extended influence for good during many years. For fourteen years he held the pastorate of the Byron church, and preached for four years at Clarendon, Orleans Co. NY. He received very little remuneration for his services, believing, "freely you have received; freely give."

He represented the Holland Purchase Y.M., in the General Conferences of 1833, 1835, and 1844, the Ohio and Pennsylvania Y.M. in that of 1841, and the Genesee Y.M. in 1853.

He had a sixty-six year ministry and died loved and esteemed, at 91 years of age.

### David Valoy Ross

Birth:
1831
Death:
September 6, 1878
Burial:
Forest Lawn Cemetery
Buffalo
Erie County, New York

When five years of age with his parents he moved from Pennsylvania to Clermont, Ohio. In 1861 he entered the Civil War and received an Hon. discharge at the end of three years. He began preaching with the Methodists, but joined the Free Baptists in 1876 and was ordained by the Miami Quarterly Meeting in Ohio the

January before his death. His many qualities endeared him to all.

### Benjamin Rowland
Birth:
Unknown
Death:
Aug. 3, 1872
Sherburne, N.Y.,
Burial:
Christ Church Cemetery
Sherburne, Chenango County,
New York

Rowland, a native of Lyme, Conn., died at age 88 years. Having moved to Burlington, N. Y., he was converted in 1812, three years after his marriage to Miss Seraph Sweetser, and almost immediately began to preach. The next year he was ordained, entering at once upon a seven years' pastorate with the Burlington and Exeter churches. In 1821 he took charge of the Sherburne church, just organized, and remained with it seventeen years, preaching also to other churches. The churches at Oneonta, Plainfield, Brookfield, Holmesville, Oxford, Lebanon, Smyrna, German Flats, and Columbus were also recipients of his labors, some of them for years. He labored extensively as an evangelist, at one period for seven consecutive years continually in revivals. In 1854 he went to Binghamton, remaining there ten years, and preaching to the Apalachin, Warren, Windham, and Vestal churches. After this he made his home in Sherburne. He was a man of arduous labors. His name was a household word over a large section of country. His baptisms numbered over eight hundred. His preaching was descriptive and hortative. He seemed to embrace the truth with the heart more than the head. He "was an advocate of temperance, a lover of education and missions. His ministry was a ministry of love.

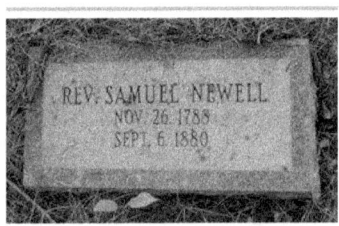

### Rev Samuel Newell
Birth:
1788
Barnstead, New York
Death:
Sep. 6, 1880
Lawrence
Nassau County, New York
Burial:
Mound Hill Cemetery
Nicholville, St. Lawrence County
New York, USA
Plot: 290-7
He served in the Legislature from Woodstock and was converted in

1831, at Johnstown, Canada, where he began to preach with the Methodists. In 1837 he settled in Lawrence, NY where he joined the Free Baptists. An ordained Free Baptist minister, died aged 91 yrs. Spouse was Polly Erwin. His ministry was mostly confined to the Lawrence, Hopkinton and Dickinson churches. He was a logical and instructive preacher, and a most exemplary Christian; and even after he had passed his fourscore years, he was listened to with interest.

### Rev George J Scobey
Birth:
Aug. 22, 1854
Buffalo
Erie County,New York
Death:
1934
Iowa
Burial:
Hillside Cemetery
Stephentown
Rensselaer County,New York

Rev. George J. SCOBEY, son of Geo. V. and F.E. (French) SCOBEY, was born at Buffalo N.Y. Aug. 22, 1853(sic). He yielded his heart to God in Feb. 1876, received license in 1880 and was ordained June 10, 1883.

### James Sharp
Birth:
Unknown
Death:

May, 18, 1874
Fairport, N. Y.
Burial:
Mount Hope Cemetery
Rochester, Monroe County,
New York

A native of Massachusetts, he died at age 76 years. He was converted in youth, his early labors being with the Methodists, much of the time in Canada. The latter part of life he was connected with the Free Baptists in western New York as a pioneer Freewill Baptist minister in Monroe County. Possessing a vigorous intellect, some culture, strong willpower and persistence, with a personal address imposing for a colored person, he had influence with the abolitionist leaders, especially with Gerritt Smith, and took great interest in the progress of their work. The visions of his earlier years were realized in the emancipation of his race (being Black) and in the gift of the elective franchise. He ceased not to thank God for the privilege of labor in this cause and for the results attained.

### Rev George H Siver
Birth:
Jan. 6, 1814
Herkimer County, New York
Death:
Sep. 15, 1891
Burial:
Garrison Cemetery, Pitcairn
St. Lawrence County,New York

Rev. George H. Siver, was born in

Herkimer County, N.Y., and married Eliza Ostrander, Sept. 22, 1834. He served for many years as a licensed preacher in connection with the Diana church of the Jefferson Quarterly Meeting (N.Y.) and about 1870 received ordination, his subsequent ministry being with the Pitcairn church

**Cyrus Steere**
Birth:
Jun. 3, 1801
Glocester
Providence County,
Rhode Island
Death:
Feb. 26, 1878
East McDonough
Chenango County, New York
Burial:
Steere Cemetery

East McDonough
Chenango County, New York

First pastor of the Free Will Baptist Church, erected in 1831 in East McDonough. Organized churches of the same denomination at German Hollow in 1844 and in Oxford in 1848. Steere, was a native of Burrillville, R. I., began his ministerial labors when twenty-six years of age, and was ordained at East McDonough, N. Y., Aug. 26, 1829. He was a pioneer in the vicinity and assisted in building up and organizing many churches. His labors were chiefly in the McDonough Q. M., and were greatly blessed. He died at aged 76 years

**George B Southwick**
Birth:
November 22, 1863
Humphrey Ctr., New York
Death:
1923
Burial:
Cherry Creek Central Cemetery
Cherry Creek
Chautauqua County, New York
Plot: 252

He graduated from Pike Seminary, New York in 1885 and student at Bates College and Cobb Divinity School. He received his license to preach in April 1885 pastoring thereafter in New York and Maine.

## Thomas A. Stevens
Birth:
April 11, 1837
Death:
1912 Burial:
Keuka Park Cemetery
Jerusalem
Yates County, New York

Ordained to preach 1868 in Plymouth, Vt. Where he ministered in that state, then to N.Y. ending with Keuka College, 1891-1901 where he died and was buried. He was a delegate to the General Conference in 1870.He was also an ordnance office in the army for three years.

## Anna Matteson Stone
Birth:
Aug. 26, 1813
Burlington
Otsego County, New York
Death:
Apr. 26, 1895
Oxford
Chenango County, New York
Burial:
Riverview Cemetery
Oxford
Chenango County, New York

Her parents were John D and Philura Williams Matteson her mother being a descendant Roger Williams. She was married Joshua B Stone Feb 5 1840 and several years after his death on Dec 22 1869 to Lewis B Anderson. She received a good education and in early engaged in teaching. She was when eighteen years of age and after few years with the Baptists united with the Free Baptists in Columbus, NY. She received license to preach about 1839 and for years engaged actively in ministerial work. While pastor she exchanged with other ministers for the administration of the ordinances. Though successful as a pastor her chief labors were as an evangelist. Her work was mostly in Madison, Chenango, and Cortland counties, NY though extending also as far as Pennsylvania and Rhode Island. Sometimes alone sometimes with other ministers she called sinners to repentance. The conversions under her labors numbering several hundreds. Her voice was clear and full not boisterous. Her manner in the pulpit was deliberate and dignified, her style hortatory yet with method and her appeals often thrilling.

**Rev Freeborn W Straight**
Birth:
1806
Washington County, New York
Death:
Dec. 23, 1878
Monroe County, New York
Burial:
Beach Ridge Cemetery
Brockport
Monroe County, New York
Plot: B.R. II 165

Soon after his birth in 1806, with his father, William Straight, moved to Walworth, Wayne Co. NY. When about twenty-one years of age he was converted under the labors of Eld. Lyon and united with the Walworth Free Baptist church. In about a year he was licensed to preach and soon after, with Elder

Marks [David], he went to Ontario, Can., where they traveled and labored with great success. Marks, returning, he remained in Canada and supplied the Woodstock and London churches, forty miles apart, and preached at intervening points. More than a hundred were converted during the winter, and he was sent to New York for ordination in March 1828. He remained in Canada several years and churches were formed which grew to become the Ontario Yearly Meeting. Returning to New York, he was inactive for a time. In 1841, he took up the work and a year later he assisted Brother Bathrick at Conneaut, Ohio, and Bro. Dunn at Mecca, many being converted at each place. He was pastor at Conneaut two years, assisted in a great revival in Pennfield, N.Y., and settled as pastor of the church at Fairport for eight years. In the winter of 1851-52 he assisted Bro. Bathrick again at Saco, ME, and more than four hundred were converted in the congregation, the revival being one of unusual power and extending also to other congregations and towns. He seemed almost inspired in his labors here. A part of the following winter was spent in revival work in Saco. After a year at Brockport, he settled at Manchester, N.H., where he remained for three years, and eighty were converted the first winter. After one year at Boston, MA, and two at Saco ME he went to Conneaut OH in 1861, and two years later to Jackson, Mich. He remained there nine years, reorganizing the church and carrying it through many difficulties. He then made his home in Lansing, intending to rest, but could not. He gathered fragments of several churches together at Grand Ledge, encouraged them to build their beautiful brick church, and by his visits aided the churches at Reading, Cambridge, Paw Paw, Bath, Macon, Delta and Leslie. Then in 1877, visiting the scene of his early labors in Ontario, he took charge of two churches in Zorra, and worked with the zeal and ardor of his youth until his sudden death, Dec. 23, 1878. Brother Straight was a man of large and commanding form, and of robust health, rather diffident unless aroused by some exigency, pre-eminently social and companionable. His intellect was of a high order, quick, discriminating and logical. He was several times a member of the General Conference. He died at the post of duty near where he preached his first sermon fifty-one years before, and was buried at Brockport, N.Y., near the scenes of his early ministry

**Ezra P Tallman**
Birth:
May 31, 1814
Death:
Aug. 21, 1867
Burial:
Elmwood Cemetery
Perrinton, Monroe County,
New York

Tallman was a native of Galway, N. Y., united with the Penfield church in his twenty-third year, and was ordained when twenty-eight. He became pastor of the Perrinton (Fairport) church, formed at the time of his ordination, and remained with it four years. He then spent nearly three years at the Biblical School at Whitestown, and afterwards was pastor of the Middleville and Norway, Byron, Penfield, and Elba and Alabama churches successively. After caring for his father, Deacon Tallman, in his last sickness, he preached occasionally, and died aged 53 years. He was highly esteemed by his brethren, and his preaching was well adapted to develop spirituality and to establish gospel principles among the people.

**William Taylor**
Birth:
Mar. 20, 1823
Ontario,
Canada
Death:
Apr. 4, 1877
Italy
Yates County, New York
Burial:
Italy-Naples Cemetery
Italy
Yates County, New York

He married Elizabeth Bodine in 1844 and Mary Morse in 1850 and had 10 children. He came to God in 1841 and was ordained in 1858. His labors were in Ontario, Canada, Western New York and Michigan. He aided in building several meeting houses and baptized several hundred converts in represented the St. Joseph's yearly meeting in the General Conference of 1883.

**Charles Luther Vail**
Birth:
Oct. 21, 1806
Long Island, New York
Death:
Dec. 23, 1887
Windsor, New York
Burial:
West Windsor Cemetery
West Windsor
Broome County, New York

He was 20 at his conversion and joined the church in West Windsor. Here he was ordained on November 3, 1840. His pastorates were West Windsor, New York, South Killingsly Connecticut and Franklin, Oxford, Virgil and Dryden, New York. He continued in active service until 73 years of age.

**Freeman VanAmburgh**
Birth:
May 1, 1793
Fishkill,
Dutchess County,
New York
Death:
Aug. 3, 1871
Bath, Steuben County, New York
Burial:
Mount Washington Cemetery
Urbana, Steuben County,
New York

Rev. Freeman VanAmburgh, is listed in names of deceased ministers in the "Register of Freewill Baptists", as having "d. Aug. 3, 1871, age 78 yrs, at Bath, N.Y."He was in the War of 1812, proven as his wife, Anna, filed a widow's pension on his service in Capt. Ellis Co., N.Y. Mil., #URS orig 44506.Rev. VanAmburgh settled a few years after his military service at Bath, where he remained for most of life. He was converted in 1824 along with others under the labors of Rev. Z. Dean, and later was organized into a Freewill Baptist church. He was ordained on Sept. 4, 1836, and continued a faithful laborer until strength and life failed.

### William Van Tuyl
Birth:
Unknown
Death:
Feb. 21, 1829
Burial:
Raplee Family Cemetery
Milo
Yates County, New York
Early Free Will Baptist preacher.

### Elder Alverdo Wait
Birth:
Mar. 23, 1805
Death:
Aug. 13, 1849
Burial:
Lower Cincinnatus Cemetery
Cincinnatus
Cortland County
New York,

He began preaching in 1844, and ordained by Freewill Bapt. McDonough Quarterly Meeting June 3, 1848. Elder/Rev. Alverdo WAIT, was an ordained Freewill Baptist minister, who ministered in his short lifetime in Cortland Co. He was interested in benevolent work, was active yet unassuming, and labored with the Cincinnatus and Cortlandville FWB churches until his death.

### Orrin Wynant Waldron
Birth:
Jul. 13, 1859
North Creek,
Warren County, New York
Death:
1910
Burial:
Ames Cemetery, Ames,
Montgomery County, New York

He consecrated his life to God in 1878, and was educated at Hillsdale College, Michigan, in the college and theological departments, receiving honors from his literary society for excellence in oratory. While in college he supplied the churches at Scipio, Litchfield and Hadley's Corners, and afterwards became pastor of the church at Marion, Ohio, receiving ordination Oct. 12, 1884 in the Free Will Baptist. After a successful pastorate of three years he entered upon the work with the church at Saco, Me. He has baptized about thirty converts and assisted in revival work. Aug. 5, 1884, he was married to Mary E. Phillips.

### Rev Russell Way
Birth:
1780
Death:
Jul. 23, 1848
Burial:
Collinsville Cemetery
Turin
Lewis County
New York

Rev. Russell Way died aged 69 years. He was converted when about twenty years of age. In 1815 he was ordained.
In his early ministry he gathered the Turin church. And remained its pastor to the end of a long and honored life. He was a ready speaker, an efficient and judicious pastor, a safe counselor and an ardent friend of the benevolent enterprises of the denomination.
Inscription:
age 68 years

### Hiram Whitcher

Birth:
Mar. 18, 1809
Danville, Caledonia County, Vermont
Death:
Jun. 7, 1896
Sweden Center, Monroe County, New York
Burial:
Lakeview Cemetery, Brockport, Monroe County, New York, Plot: A-111-1

The family moved to Sweden, NY in 1815. Here in 1823, Hiram was converted and uniting with the Union Free Baptist Church of Sweden and Ogden. He received from it a license to preach in 1829. During the summer he was chiefly engaged in study and attended the Middlebury academy. In the spring, he assisted Elder T. Parker in a glorious revival at Penfield and soon joined the church there, after which he was ordained May 30, 1830, by a council of the Bethany Quarterly Meeting. In 1831, he went into Chautauqua County and held revivals in many places and also in Cataraugua County. Many converts were baptized, among them Miss Lavina Crawford and Miss H. Baldwin later to become missionaries, and also Dr. Kingsley, later a bishop of the M.E. church. He held meetings in Ohio, Michigan, and Pennsylvania. In 1834 he settled at Springville and entered the academy, preaching also in the vicinity. In 1840, he with

others served as a committee from the General Conference to arrange a union with the Free Communion Baptists. He preached also at Clinton, Poland, Unadilla Forks, and Whitestown, NY. From 1845 to 1854, he labored in Rochester, NY. From there he went to Concord, NH under direction of the Home Mission Society. The following twenty years were spent in Maine, at Booth Bay, Bath, Augusta, Phillips, Falmouth, Saccarappa and elsewhere. After fifty years of active service he accepted a home provided by his brother, C.J. Whitcher, and moved to Brockport, NY, from which place he has rendered service to several churches. During his ministry, Bro. Whitcher has been engaged in many revivals, and has baptized 680 converts.

### William Whitfield

Birth:
December 27, 1811
London, England
Death:
1891
Burial:
Pierpont Hill Cemetery

Pierpont
St. Lawrence County, New York
He was converted in September 1830 receiving license eight years later and ordination on June 14, 1841. He assisted in organizing the Pierpoint and several other churches. And with the exception of two years in the Jefferson Quarterly Meeting, he has resided at Pierpoint ministering to the people. For 16 years he was clerk of the town and has been for 37 years clerk of the St. Lawrence Yearly Meeting. Among its churches he is had wide influence. He joined in marriage 387 couples. In 1831 he was married to Diantha M. Axtell.

### Edwin E. Whittemore
Birth:
Nov. 26, 1850
Oneida County, New York
Death:
1932
Burial:
Prospect Cemetery
Prospect
Oneida County, New York

He married Ellen M. Myers, August 1, 1876. He was educated at Whitestown Seminary, and was principal of the Prospect School six years. He was appointed as village clerk at Prospect. After a religious awakening he turned to God in March 1873, and after serving one year as a licentiate, was ordained by the Whitestown (NY) Quarterly Meeting. He held pastorates at Prospect, Grant and Unadilla Forks and has supplied elsewhere.

### Philip Wight
Birth:
Aug. 26, 1793
New Hampshire
Death:
Mar. 11, 1853
Hornby
Steuben County
New York
Burial:
Beaver Dams Cemetery
Beaver Dams
Schuyler County, New York

"Rev. Phillip Wight, a native of New Hampshire, died in Hornby, N.Y., March 11, 1853, aged 60 years. He commenced preaching with the Free Baptists when thirty years of age, and after gathering the Milan church, was ordained as an evangelist in 1826.
In 1836 he removed to New York. He was a faithful advocate of the reforms of the day, and his labors were blessed."--from the "Free Baptist Cyclopedia, pub. 1889, by Burgess and Ward.

His parents were Daniel and Hannah (Lyon) WIGHT, his father being of Revolution War fame. Rev. Wight married Dorcus Hibbard, about 1810, the daughter of John and Sarah Hibbard, of Mass. They had several children, which names are shown on 1850 NY census.

**John Wilcox**
Birth:
1776
Death:
Feb. 19, 1863
Burial:
Bemis Cemetery
Antwerp
Jefferson County
New York

A Free Baptist minister ordained after June 1796.Died at 86 years, 11 months & 29 days. Husband of Mary Wilcox.

Military Service:
WAR OF 1812 Ballengers Reg., NY Militia.

**Rev John Wilcox**
Birth:
Nov. 12, 1760
Westerly
Washington County
Rhode Island
Death:
Jul., 1835
Allegany County
New York
Burial:
Wheeler Cemetery
Wirt
Allegany County
New York

He went from RI to Petersburg, NY, where he united with the church at its organization, June 18, 1796. He was subsequently ordained.

# *Death provides the saint to partake of the refreshing of the soul.*

**Rev Noah D Wilkins**
Birth:
Jun., 1806
New York
Death:
Apr. 21, 1871
New York
Burial:
North Afton Cemetery
Afton
Chenango County, New York

An ordained Free Baptist minister from NY, whose name appears in the General Conf. Minutes, in a list of their ministers who had died in 1871.

**Joseph Wilson**
Birth:
July 8,.1808
German Flats, N. Y.
Death:
Nov. 12, 1878
Gilbert's Mills, N. Y.
Burial:
Gilbert Mills Cemetery
Pennellville, Oswego County, New York

His spiritual life began in 1835, and he soon received license to preach. In 1840 he was ordained. He was pastor at Granby four years, at German Flats six years, witnessing a gracious outpouring of the spirit, at Gilbert's Mills six years, and also preached in Hastings, Constantia, West Monroe, Parish and other places.He preached a full gospel and was abundant in labors of love. Aug. 29, 1829, he married Ruth Thomas, of German Flats. Benjamin Randall was a great-uncle of Mrs. Wilson.

**Amos Wing**
Birth:
Nov. 29, 1796
Saratoga County, New York
Death:
Jun. 29, 1879
Oneonta, N.Y
Burial:
Oneonta Plains Cemetery
Oneonta, Otsego County, New York, Plot: Old Section

Son of John and Sylvia Wing. He was Free Baptist clergyman for 45 years in the Freewill Baptist denomination in various places. History of Second Freewill Baptist, Oneonta, shows that he founded it, and pastored it. He was married on

Nov. 12, 1820, to Chloe Lyon, b. 26 June, 1801, and d. 25 April 1823. In 1822 he married a second time to Lucinda R. Newman, b. 26 June 1801, and died 1887. Rev. Amos Wing, died at age 82 years. He was born in Saratoga County, but when young moved to Burlington, where he was baptized by Elder William Hunt. He soon began to preach and spent the remainder of his long life in the ministry, being connected many years with the Oneonta church of the Otsego Quarterly Meeting. He was a good man and God blessed his labors

### Joseph Wood
Birth:
1809
Death:
May 3, 1878
Naples, N. Y.
Burial:
Burns Cemetery
Burns, Allegany County, New York

For nearly thirty years he was devoted to the work of the ministry. He preached for some twelve churches in western New York, and in nearly every instance good results were manifest. He was a man of excellent judgment and a good minister. The Genesee Y. M. made him a member of the General Conference at Fairport in 1877. His only son fell at Gettysburg.
Inscription:
Age 69 Years
(Civil War Vet)

### Ray Woodmansee
Birth:
1794
Death:
Dec. 13, 1875
South New Berlin, N. Y.
Burial:
Riverside Cemetery
South New Berlin,
Chenango County, New York

Woodmansee died at age 8l years. He was son of Joseph Woodmansee, of Richmond, R. I., and received ordination with the Reformed Methodists in 1836. In 1845 he moved to New Berlin, N. Y., and soon joined the Holmesville Free Baptist church and was their pastor several years. With the infirmities of age he retired from the pulpit, but gave the influence of his sweet-spirited life to the cause. He loved every cause that honored God and promoted religion.

# Death Is The Entry To Life Evermore

### Dyer Woodworth
Birth:
Jan. 26, 1798
New York
Death:
Feb. 2, 1859
Burial:
West Hill Cemetery
Hornby
Steuben County, New York

After joining the Calvinistic Baptists when 22 years of age and studying three years in Madison University in preparation for the ministry, he became a Free Baptists in 1840 and was ordained the following year. He was pastor of the Free Baptist Church at Addison, New York for nine years. While living he gave for benevolent purposes about $4000 and he perpetuated his influence by the bequeathing $8000 to the Free Baptist Foreign Mission Societies and the American Bible Society. In his pulpit ministrations he was clear, argumentative and impressive.

### William W Young
Birth:
Sep. 22, 1813
Parma
Monroe County, New York
Death:
Oct. 5, 1884
Morganville
Genesee County,
New York
Burial:

Morganville Cemetery
Stafford
Genesee County,
New York

He was converted in youth and uniting with the Clarkson church, soon began to preach. About 1836, Elders D.(David) Marks, J. N. Hinckley and E. Hannibal, ordained him.

His labors were mostly with the churches of the Monroe and Rochester Quarterly Meetings. His sermons were plain and instructive, and many embraced redemption through his instrumentality.

His parents were Eli Montgomery Young and Temperance Palmer.

He married Hester Ann Knapp, 22 June 1837, in Knapps Corner, NY. at age 23.

# PIONEER FREE WILL BAPTISTS MINISTERS BURIAL LOCATIONS IN NEW YORK

www.ingramcontent.com/pod-product-compliance
Lightning Source LLC
Chambersburg PA
CBHW070837310526
45788CB00017B/1472